# Involuntary manslaughter

# Part of '*The Law Explained*' series

### (including a review of *actus reus, mens rea* and murder)

## Sally Russell LLB (Hons), PGCE

My main objective has been to combine legal accuracy with a style that is accessible to all students, so I hope you will find this book both stimulating and helpful. Fully updated with recent cases and laws it is written in a lively, clear and accessible way and is designed to help students of all learning styles to understand the subject.

Although aimed at A-Level the books provide a good base for 1st Year LLB, ILEX and other courses, and can be used as self-study guides.

Each Chapter contains **examples** to help you see how the law relates to real life situations; **tasks** and **self-test questions**, to help you check your understanding, as well as **examination tips** and **application practice** to help you prepare for problem questions. Where applicable the books also contain **tips and guidance on evaluating** the law to help with essay questions. **Summaries** and **diagrams** help to make the law clear and the **'must-know' cases are highlighted**. Answers are given for the tasks and self-test questions either in the book or on my website at www.drsr.org

The '*the law explained*' series offers a more in-depth coverage of individual areas with additional tasks, examples and examination practice. This means you can pick those topics for which you need more guidance (all the answers are included in the book).

**For a range of free interactive exercises please go to www.drsr.org and click on 'Free Exercises' to see what's available.**

### Other books by Sally Russell

As new books may be available by the time you read this I have not listed my other books by title. They currently include crime and tort at AS level, crime, tort and concepts of law for both the AQA and OCR examination board at A2 level and various books in '*the law explained*' series. For the most up to date list of what is available please check my author's page on Amazon or visit my website at www.drsr.org. All my books are available in both Kindle and paperback format.

### About the author

Sally Russell was formerly head of law at a sixth-form college, a senior examiner for AQA and tort advisor for the Institute of Legal Executive Tutorial College. She has written various materials for both teachers and students, for Pearson Education, Hodder education and the National Extension College. She is also a regular contributor to the A-Level Law Review. For more information visit www.drsr.org

# Table of contents

Involuntary manslaughter is a term used to distinguish between cases where there is no *mens rea* for murder so the charge is manslaughter, and cases where there is *mens rea*, so the charge is murder, but there is a defence, which makes it 'voluntary' manslaughter rather than murder.

There are two types of (involuntary) manslaughter. These are gross negligence manslaughter (including the possibility of reckless manslaughter) and constructive manslaughter (also called unlawful act manslaughter). The main substance of this booklet is these two types of manslaughter. However, I have repeated a little on *actus reus* and *mens rea* as a reminder of these issues as they apply to involuntary manslaughter. Manslaughter is a result crime so causation is very important. As for *mens rea,* it is where intent is not proven that makes the crime manslaughter rather than murder.

### Example

Kylie is in Mike's car when he suddenly pulls out a knife and threatens to rape her. She jumps out in fright and a passing bus hits her. She dies a few days later in hospital.

Intent would be hard to prove because Mike's purpose was to rape her not to seriously injure her, so a murder charge is likely to fail. However, his act was unlawful and it caused death because (as in **Roberts**) Kylie's act of jumping out is foreseeable and reasonable and so is unlikely to break the chain of causation. This will be constructive or unlawful act manslaughter.

If Kylie's injuries were not life threatening, but she later died from poor hospital treatment, this would also be unlikely to break the chain of causation (as confirmed in **Cheshire**). However, if she was only slightly hurt and the treatment she received was so grossly negligent that she died, then the chain could be broken. In this case, the doctor who treated her could be guilty of gross negligence manslaughter. There is no need for an unlawful act for this type of manslaughter, only criminal negligence.

The tasks are intended to reinforce your learning so do these as you go along. The answers are at the end of the book. Some tasks will just ask you to jot down a few thoughts for use in an essay question, so there are no answers to these, but keep your notes for revision and exam practice. I have included occasional quotes so use these too; they show that you know what judges have to say about the law.

**There are also some free interactive exercises at www.drsr.org**

A brief reminder: Criminal cases are usually in the form *R v the defendant*. It is acceptable to use just the name so if the case is **R v Miller** I have called it **Miller**. If another form is used, e.g., **DPP v Miller** I have used the full title, as you may want to look up the case for further information. Civil cases are between the *claimant* and the *defendant*, although you will see the word *'plaintiff'* in cases before 1999.

There is a list of some common abbreviations in the appendix at the end of the booklet.

**Actus reus**

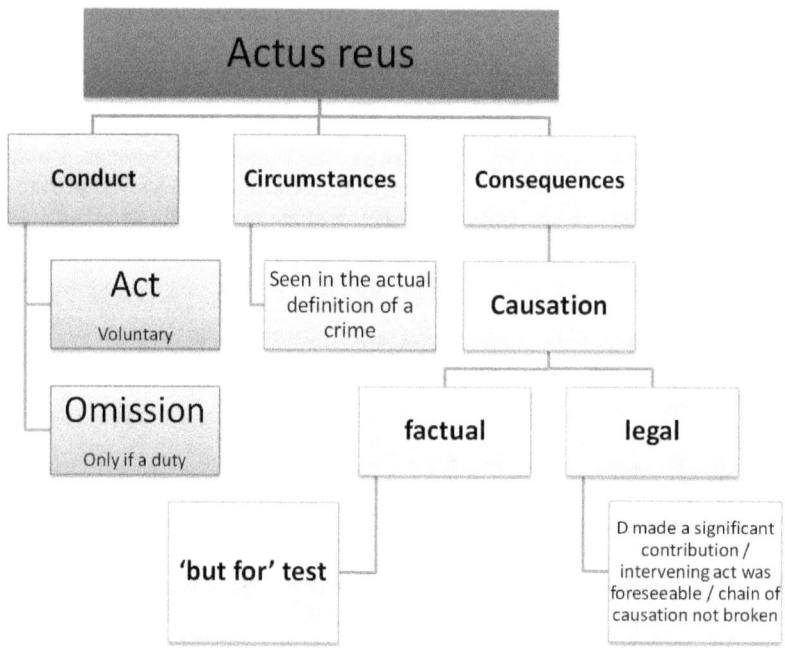

In most crimes, the act must be voluntary.

An omission, or failure to act, can amount to the *actus reus* if there is a duty to act.  In all the following cases, a failure to act resulted in a death.

In **Pittwood 1902**, D had a contractual duty to shut the railway crossing gate so was guilty of manslaughter when he failed to do so.

In **Stone and Dobinson 1977**, a couple had a voluntary duty to care for a relative so were guilty of manslaughter for failing to do so.

In **Evans 2009**, D had created a dangerous situation by supplying drugs to her half-sister.  She therefore had a duty to take steps to remedy the situation (as in **Miller**) so was guilty of manslaughter for failing to do so.

All three of these cases were manslaughter, specifically gross negligence manslaughter.  This is the only type of manslaughter that can be committed by an omission rather than a positive act.

Crimes where a particular consequence is part of the *actus reus* are called **result crimes**.  For manslaughter, death must result from (be caused by) D's act or omission.  The prosecution must prove causation both **factually** and **legally**.

Factual causation is proved using the 'but for' test.  For murder the prosecution must show that 'but for' D's conduct, the victim would not have died.

**Key case**

In **White 1910**, D put cyanide in a drink intending to kill his mother, who was found dead shortly afterwards with the drink 3 parts full.  In fact, the mother had died of a heart attack unconnected with the poison.  The son was found not guilty of murder.  He had the *mens rea* (he intended to kill her) but not the *actus reus* (his act didn't cause her death). He was guilty of attempted murder, however.

Legal causation is based on the 'chain of causation'. There must be an unbroken link, or chain, between D's action and the death. When something has occurred after D's original act, then it may be argued that the chain of causation is broken.

**Key case**

In **Cheshire 1991**, due to negligent treatment by the hospital, the victim of a shooting died. The court held that as long as D's action was a **'significant and operative'** cause of the death it need not be the sole cause. Hospital treatment will not break the chain unless it is *"so **independent of D's acts** and in itself so **potent in causing death**, that the contribution made by D is insignificant."* Thus, if D makes a significant contribution to the death this is enough, even if there are other causes as well.

The courts rarely allow medical treatment to break the chain of causation. The principle from **Cheshire** was followed by the CA in **Mellor 1996**, where failure to give proper treatment contributed to the death of the victim of an attack, but D was found guilty of his murder.

In **Pagett 1983**, D fired a shotgun at armed police while holding a girl hostage in front of him. They returned fire, killing the girl. The court held that the actions of the police did not break the chain because shooting back was a 'natural consequence' of his having shot first. This is based on the principle from **Roberts 1971** that a foreseeable act does not break the chain. In **Roberts**, D assaulted a girl who then jumped out of a moving car, and was injured. It was held that only if it was something that no reasonable person could foresee would the chain of causation be broken by the victim's actions. In **Williams & Davis 1992**, the CA said that the chain of causation is not broken unless V does something *"so daft or unexpected"* that no reasonable person could foresee it.

**Examination tip**

It may be difficult to decide what acts should be considered 'independent' or 'potent' enough to break the causation chain or what amounts to a 'daft' act by the victim. There can be a thin line between doing 'something wrong in the agony of the moment' and doing something 'daft'. The main thing is to be logical. State the law from **Cheshire** and **Roberts** on these issues and apply it to the facts given. If someone does something that hastens death which seems independent of D's act, or the victim does something wholly unpredictable, then go on to say that this could break the chain of causation so that D is not liable for the death.

## Coincidence of *actus reus* and *mens rea*

Although *actus reus* and *mens rea* must coincide, the court may view the *actus reus* as continuing or as a 'series' of acts.

In **Fagan v Metropolitan Police Commissioner 1969**, D accidentally drove onto a police officer's foot and then refused to move. The court held there was a continuing act (*actus reus*) up until the refusal to move (*mens rea*) therefore the two coincided.

In **Thabo Meli 1954**, the Ds tried to kill a man and rolled his body over a cliff. As it happened, he wasn't dead and the actual cause of death was exposure. The Ds argued that the first act (the attack), although done with *mens rea,* was not the cause of death (so no *actus reus*). The second act (pushing him over the cliff) was the cause of death, but was not accompanied by *mens rea* as they thought he was already dead. The court said that it was *"impossible to divide up what was really one series of acts* in this way"*.

## The 'thin skull' rule

The chain is not broken by a particular vulnerability in the victim. Lawton LJ said in **Blaue 1975**, *"those who use violence on other people must take their victims as they find them"*. Also known as the 'thin-skull rule', it means that if a particular disability in the victim makes them more likely to die, D is still liable. The 'disability' is usually physical (such as a pre-existing medical condition like a 'thin skull') but in **Blaue** it was the fact that she was a Jehovah's Witness and so refused to have a blood transfusion.

**Pagett** and **Blaue** are examples of unlawful act manslaughter. This requires a positive and unlawful act. In these cases, the unlawful acts were shooting at the police and stabbing the girl respectively. In both cases the unlawful act caused death because the chain was neither broken by the police returning fire nor by the girl refusing a blood transfusion.

### Mens rea

The term *mens rea* refers to the state of mind of the accused at the time the *actus reus* is committed. As we saw *mens rea* and *actus reus* must exist at the same time.

The two main types of *mens rea* are intention and recklessness.

It is important to be able to identify both the *actus reus* and the *mens rea* of the offence when answering a problem question because every part of a crime has to be proved. As we saw in **White**, if part of the *actus reus* or *mens rea* is not proved, D is not guilty of the offence.

Many cases dealing with intention are homicide cases because intention differentiates murder from manslaughter. The *mens rea* for manslaughter is unusual in that it is the *mens rea* for the unlawful act, rather than for the death. This can be intent or recklessness so we will review these briefly and look at the specific issues of *mens rea* with the topic itself in the next chapter.

## Direct Intent

Direct intent means the result is D's aim or purpose. This is what most of us would understand by intention. If you pick up a loaded gun and fire it at someone with the aim of killing them, it can be said without any difficulty that you intended to do so. Intention was defined in **Mohan 1975** as 'the decision to bring about' the result, or prohibited consequence, whether that result was desired or not. The courts have given the concept of intention a wider meaning, however. This is referred to as oblique, or indirect, intent.

## Oblique or indirect intent

Here the consequence isn't D's aim but is 'virtually certain' to occur because of D's actions.

The law on oblique intent was clarified somewhat by the HL in **Woollin 1998**, which confirmed the standard direction for the jury given by the CA in **Nedrick 1986**. This was:

> That death or serious bodily harm was a **virtual certainty** as a result of the defendant's actions and

> **the defendant appreciated** that such was the case

## Recklessness

Subjective recklessness is used for most crimes as an alternative *mens rea* to intent.

**Key case**

**Cunningham 1957** provides the test for subjective recklessness. D ripped a gas meter from a basement wall in order to steal the money in the meter. Gas escaped and seeped through to an adjoining property where an occupant was overcome by the fumes. D was charged with maliciously administering a noxious substance, and argued that he did not realise the risk of gas escaping. The

CA quashed his conviction having interpreted 'maliciously' to mean with subjective recklessness. The prosecution had failed to prove that D was aware that his actions might cause harm. The test for subjective recklessness is therefore that:

**D is aware of the existence of a risk (of the consequence occurring) and deliberately goes ahead and takes that risk.**

There were two types of recklessness but objective recklessness (which was used for criminal damage until 2003) has now been abolished. Subjective means looking at what was in the *defendant's* mind. In **Gemmell and Richards 2003,** two boys aged 11 and 13 set light to some papers outside the back of a shop. Several premises were badly damaged. They were convicted of arson based on objective recklessness, i.e., that the risk of damage was obvious to a reasonable person. Their ages were therefore not taken into account. Their appeal went to the HL, which used the **1966 Practice Statement** to overrule its previous decision in **Caldwell**. The HL confirmed that recklessness is subjective, so that the *defendant* had to have recognised that there was a risk. Therefore, *mens rea* for criminal damage as well as most other crimes is now subjective (**Cunningham**) recklessness, i.e., D is aware of a risk of damage, but deliberately goes ahead and takes it. This may be important where a problem scenario involves unlawful act manslaughter because for that crime the *mens rea* is that for the unlawful act. This could be criminal damage. An example is **Hancock and Shankland** where throwing boulders onto a taxi was criminal damage (an unlawful act) and caused the driver's death. They had been reckless in doing this so were guilty of manslaughter

### Examination tip

When applying the law on intent you need only use **Nedrick** and **Woollin**, and only then in cases of oblique intent, not where it is direct. This was made clear in **Woollin**. D's knowledge will be an important factor. Look carefully at the facts for information such as 'they knew that ...' or 'unknown to them ...'. These comments will help you to decide whether intent is direct or indirect and to apply the test if necessary to conclude whether there is intent at all. You may need to show that intent is hard to prove so the appropriate charge is manslaughter. If applying the law on recklessness you only need to discuss subjective (**Cunningham**) recklessness. This is now the law as confirmed by the HL in **Gemmell**.

### Transferred Malice

*Mens rea* can be transferred from the intended victim to the actual victim. This means that if you intend to hit Steve but miss and hit Joe you cannot say 'but I didn't intend to hit Joe so I had no *mens rea*'. In **Latimer 1886**, D aimed a blow at X with his belt but missed and seriously wounded V. He had the intent (*mens rea*) to hit X, and this intent was transferred to the wounding (*actus reus*) of V. Thus, he had both the *mens rea* and the *actus reus* of wounding. If V had died the charge could have been murder or manslaughter. However, the *actus reus* and *mens rea* must be for the *same* crime.

For some free interactive exercises visit www.drsr.org and click on Free Exercises to see what's available

*Gross negligence manslaughter*

This type of manslaughter occurs when someone owes a duty to another person, but is 'grossly negligent', with the result that the person dies.

**Example**

A ferry captain gets drunk and the ferry hits a rock and sinks, killing several passengers. He will be charged with gross negligence manslaughter because he owed a duty of care to his passengers, and getting so drunk whilst in charge of a ferry is likely to be sufficiently negligent.

The rules on gross negligence manslaughter were clarified by the HL in **Adomako 1994**.

**Key case**

In **Adomako**, an anaesthetist had failed to monitor a patient during an operation. The patient later died as a result. The doctor was accused of manslaughter.

The CA held that in order to prove gross negligence manslaughter there must be:

**A risk of death**

**A duty of care**

**Breach of that duty**

**Gross negligence as regards that breach, which must be sufficient to justify criminal liability**

The CA also gave examples of the type of conduct which might amount to such negligence. When the case went to the HL, the test was confirmed but the HL rejected the idea of setting out particular examples. Lord Mackay said that the jury would have to decide whether "*involving as it must have done a risk of death*" D's conduct fell below the standard expected to the extent "*that it should be judged criminal*". On the facts, this was the case and the conviction was upheld.

It seemed that this replaced reckless manslaughter, which Lord Mackay said in **Adomako** no longer existed. However, he also said, "*I consider it perfectly appropriate that the word reckless be used in cases of involuntary manslaughter*". This left the matter somewhat uncertain.

In **Khan and Khan 1998**, the CA said that there were only **two** types of involuntary manslaughter: unlawful act manslaughter and gross negligence manslaughter. This apparently confirmed **Adomako**, that reckless manslaughter no longer existed. However, doubt was again cast on this in **Lidar 2000**.

In **Lidar**, a group of men had a fight in the car park of a pub. When two of them got in a car and started to drive off, a third leant in the window of the car and the fight continued. They drove off with him half in the window and at some point he fell off and suffered injuries from which he died. The jury were directed in terms of recklessness and the driver was convicted of manslaughter. The CA upheld the conviction, possibly relying on Lord Mackay's reference in **Adomako** to it being "perfectly appropriate" to use the word reckless. A driver owes a duty to other road users, and his recklessness in driving with someone hanging on to the car would be covered by the term gross negligence. A finding of gross negligence manslaughter would have therefore been possible, so it is the rules from **Adomako** that are important to know.

**The requirements for gross negligence manslaughter**

The **Adomako** requirements were confirmed in **Misra 2004**.

### Key case

In **Misra**, also a medical negligence case, it was argued that the uncertainty in the law of gross negligence manslaughter meant that it infringed the **European Convention on Human Rights**. The CA rejected this argument and held that the offence had been sufficiently clearly set out in **Adomako**. Grossly negligent treatment, which exposed a patient to the risk of death, and caused death, would make the doctor liable for manslaughter.

The CA also said that it had been 'clearly established' that a risk of death was needed; a risk of bodily injury or injury to health was not enough.

As well as a **risk of death**, the death must have occurred as a result of a **breach** of a **duty** owed by D to V. Then the jury must decide whether D's breach of duty was **grossly** negligent and therefore criminal.

Let's look at these four requirements.

### Risk of death

In **Misra 2004**, the CA confirmed that a risk of death was needed, not just a risk of harm. This will still be quite wide. Activities which are dangerous in themselves, such as taking people mountaineering or white-water rafting would be included. Ordinary activities which have the potential to be dangerous could also involve a risk of death. This would cover driving a train or piloting a ferry. Such activities are not dangerous in themselves, but if a train or ferry is handled negligently or poorly maintained, there is a risk of death, so the driver or company may be liable.

### Duty

It was not made fully clear in **Adomako** whether the ordinary civil test for duty is enough. Later cases suggest that it is. In **Wacker 2003**, the Ds were transporting about 60 illegal immigrants in a lorry. For some time during the journey, there was no ventilation. Most of the immigrants died and the Ds were charged with gross negligence manslaughter. The judge referred to **Adomako** and the 'ordinary principles of the law of negligence'. This means a duty arises when a person has responsibility for another or where their actions could foreseeably cause harm to another. The CA held that they had assumed a duty of care for the victims and rejected their appeal against conviction.

### Task 1

Look back at Chapter 1 for the following manslaughter cases. What was the duty and how was it breached?

**Stone and Dobinson 1977**

**Pittwood 1902**

### Key case

**Khan and Khan** is a case worth knowing because gross negligence manslaughter, constructive manslaughter and omissions were all discussed. It also seems to confirm that there are only two types of manslaughter, so reckless manslaughter no longer exists. The Ds had supplied drugs to a young prostitute. She went into a coma but they left her and when they returned the next day, she had died. This was a failure to act, an *omission* (not getting medical help). The trial judge referred to 'manslaughter by omission' and found them guilty. The CA allowed the appeal and stated that there were only two types of involuntary manslaughter. These were unlawful act manslaughter (which requires an act, not an omission) and gross negligence manslaughter (which requires a pre-existing duty, as in **Stone and Dobinson**). The CA held that there was no such duty between a drug dealer and a client. D could not be guilty of either type of manslaughter.

In **Khan**, the CA refused to find that a duty was owed by a drug dealer to a client. However, they did suggest that such a duty *could* arise. If the facts were capable of giving rise to a duty, then the judge should give the jury *"an appropriate direction which would enable them to answer the question whether on the facts as found by them there was such a duty"*.

The CA restated this in **Evans 2009**. The judge will direct the jury as to whether the facts were *capable* of giving rise to a duty; the jury must then decide whether in fact they did so.

In **Evans**, the CA held that if a person created, or contributed to, a situation which was life threatening then a duty to take reasonable steps to save that life would arise. D had supplied heroin to her 16-year-old half-sister, who had injected it herself. When she showed symptoms of having overdosed D took no action, fearing she would get into trouble. She and her mother put the girl to bed but she was dead the next morning. They were both convicted of gross negligence manslaughter and D appealed based on the lack of a duty of care. The CA held that the duty in cases of gross negligence manslaughter was not confined to family and professional relationships. The CA noted that cases had not been clear on whether the judge or the jury should decide on whether a duty was owed. The CA held that whether a duty of care could exist was a question of law for the judge. However, it was for the jury to look at the facts to decide whether such a duty had been established. On the facts, a duty was owed and she had been grossly negligent in creating the situation and then not getting help.

### Breach of duty / the conduct amounted to gross negligence
In civil law, breach means D has not reached the standard expected of a reasonable person. However only if D is *grossly* negligent will there be criminal liability. This is for the jury to decide. According to **Adomako**, the jury must look at the circumstances and decide whether D's conduct was sufficiently grossly negligent to be deemed criminal. This was confirmed in **Misra 2004**. First there must be a breach (has D acted like a reasonable person?), then this breach must be seen by the jury as sufficiently negligent to be deemed criminal.

In **Wood and Hodgson 2003**, a 10-year-old girl was visiting the Ds. She found some ecstasy tablets in a cigarette packet and took some. There was evidence that they had hidden the tablets, and they had attempted to treat her, but they did not call an ambulance for some time. She later died in hospital. They were charged with gross negligence manslaughter.

### Task 2
Apply the rules on gross negligence manslaughter to the facts of **Wood and Hodgson**.

In **Willoughby 2004**, D was the owner of a disused public house. He had recruited a local taxi driver to help him set fire to the building for financial purposes. The taxi driver was killed when the building collapsed and D was convicted of gross negligence manslaughter. On appeal, the CA said that the judge should have directed the jury on unlawful act manslaughter rather than gross negligence manslaughter. They made it clear that either may be appropriate, depending on the circumstances. (On the facts, the jury had accepted that D had committed arson which is an unlawful act, and this caused death, so the manslaughter conviction was upheld.)

## Summary

The **Adomako** requirements as confirmed in **Misra** are:

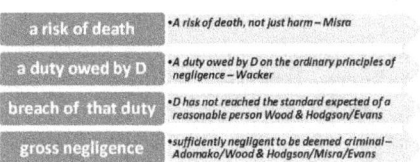

| | |
|---|---|
| **a risk of death** | •A risk of death, not just harm – Misra |
| **a duty owed by D** | •A duty owed by D on the ordinary principles of negligence – Wacker |
| **breach of that duty** | •D has not reached the standard expected of a reasonable person Wood & Hodgson/Evans |
| **gross negligence** | •sufficiently negligent to be deemed criminal – Adomako/Wood & Hodgson/Misra/Evans |

### *Constructive or unlawful act manslaughter*

This second type of manslaughter is 'constructed' from an act which is both unlawful and dangerous and which causes death. It is called both constructive manslaughter and unlawful act manslaughter.

### *Actus reus*

There are three requirements for the *actus reus*

**an unlawful act**

**which is dangerous**

**which causes death**

### Unlawful act

An act is only unlawful for the purposes of constructive manslaughter if it is a crime. Criminal damage is a common example, as in **Hancock and Shankland**. Assault is another.

In **Lamb 1967**, D pointed a loaded gun at V, his friend, as a joke. They did not understand how a revolver works, and thought that there was no danger in pulling the trigger. D did so and V died. The court said the unlawful act must be a crime and so he was not guilty.

There must be an act not an omission. In **Khan 1998**, the charge of unlawful act manslaughter failed because there was no act, just an omission to get medical help.

### Task 3

Look up these cases and identify the unlawful act. Then make a note of how causation in fact and in law is proved and how these apply.

**Hancock and Shankland 1986**

**Pagett 1983**

**Nedrick 1986**

### Which is dangerous

Whether the unlawful act is dangerous is an objective test. It was stated in **Church 1967** that

*"the unlawful act must be such as all sober and reasonable people would inevitably recognise must subject the other person to, at least, the risk of some harm resulting therefrom, albeit not serious harm".*

### Key case

In **Church**, D had knocked a woman unconscious and then, wrongly believing her to be dead, threw her in the river to dispose of the 'body'. The CA held that it did not matter that D did not see any risk of harm. In this case, D did not see any such risk as he thought she was dead. So, the principle is that if reasonable people would see the risk of harm, this will be enough. D was guilty of manslaughter because reasonable people would see that throwing someone into a river risks harm.

In **R v M (J); R v M (S) 2012**, two Ds were involved in a violent incident at a nightclub after being asked to leave. One of the doormen collapsed from shock shortly afterwards and died. The CA rejected the appeal against a manslaughter conviction and confirmed that it was not necessary for *D* to have foreseen any specific harm to the victim. What mattered was whether *'reasonable and sober people'* would have recognised that the unlawful activities subjected the victim to the risk of some harm. On the facts, it was clear that sober and reasonable people observing the events would have recognised that the doormen involved in the effort to control the Ds were at the risk of some harm.

Physical assaults will usually be deemed dangerous; unlawful acts like robbery and burglary will depend on the circumstances.

In **Dawson 1985**, during an attempted robbery of a garage, the Ds had frightened V with an imitation pistol. He suffered from a heart condition and subsequently died. They were found not guilty of manslaughter because a reasonable person would not have been aware of the heart condition, and so would not see the act as dangerous. The court recognised that fear could be foreseen, but as physical harm could not be, the act was not dangerous in the true sense.

**Dawson** was distinguished in **Watson 1989**. Burglars entered a house and saw an elderly man, but continued with their act of burglary. They were charged with manslaughter when he died of a heart attack. The man's frailty was obvious and the Ds saw this. Their knowledge could be attributed to the reasonable person who could therefore see the danger of the act, thus **Dawson** could be distinguished. (Note that on the facts their conviction was quashed on the causation issue, because there was not enough evidence that the shock of seeing burglars caused death.)

In **Bristow 2013**, a man died after intervening in a burglary at an off-road vehicle repair shop. The Ds argued that the burglary was not dangerous until after V arrived and the escape car was driven dangerously, i.e., at the time the risk of harm became apparent. At this point, there was no evidence as to who was driving so, they argued, no one was guilty. The CA held that this was not like **Dawson** or **Watson,** and although burglary was not dangerous in itself, the particular circumstances could make it so. Here the risk was obvious from the outset of the burglary because of the nature of the premises and their geography. There was a limited escape route with nearby residential accommodation. The reasonable person would see a risk of harm being caused to anyone trying to intervene or prevent escape.

**Let's review the principles which arise from these cases as regards what is dangerous**

### Examination tip

Take care when applying the rules in a problem scenario. Students often misunderstand the point of **Dawson** and confuse it with the thin skull rule. This rule may well be relevant but it will only apply once the act is found to be unlawful and dangerous. It is a causation issue. In **Dawson**, the question was whether the act was dangerous. The answer was 'no' because a reasonable person would not know of the heart condition. If the act *had* been dangerous then D would 'take the victim as he finds him'. Thus, D would be liable for the death even though a person without a heart condition would not have died.

### Example

Consider the following imaginary cases:

*1. You are angry and wave your fist at Cathy. She is of a very nervous disposition and dies of fright.*

*2. You are angry and throw a brick at Kate, which misses. She is of a very nervous disposition and dies of fright.*

In the first case, your action may be unlawful (causing fear is an assault), but is unlikely to be seen as dangerous. Much may depend on whether you know she is of a nervous disposition, if not you are not guilty of Cathy's manslaughter. It ends there.

In the second case, your act is both unlawful and dangerous. The next question is whether you caused Kate's death. You cannot argue that most people would not have died, and that Kate's nervous disposition caused her death. Under the thin skull rule, you must 'take your victim as you find her'. You are guilty of manslaughter.

### Causes death

The usual rules of causation apply, i.e., D must make a significant contribution to the death and the chain of causation must not be broken. Let's look at the cases in your task.

### Examples

**Hancock and Shankland** – throwing concrete blocks onto a taxi would be criminal damage, thus unlawful. Throwing concrete blocks off a bridge is dangerous. The unlawful act caused the driver's death because 'but for' this he would not have died and there were no intervening events to break the chain.

**Nedrick** – setting fire to something belonging to someone else is a type of criminal damage (arson) and so again unlawful. Arson is clearly dangerous and the fire caused death because 'but for' the setting of the fire she would not have died. There were also no intervening events to break the chain.

**Pagett** – shooting at the police is both unlawful and dangerous and but for this act she would not have died. D made a significant contribution to the girl's death and the police didn't break the chain of causation by firing back because it was a natural reaction (foreseeable). The shooting caused death.

Causation is not always easy to prove and problems have arisen in several cases. Compare the following two decisions.

In **Cato 1976**, D supplied, and assisted V to take, heroin which resulted in death. It was held that he had unlawfully administered a drug which caused death and so was guilty of manslaughter.

In **Dalby 1982**, the CA quashed the conviction because although D had supplied drugs (an unlawful act) this had not caused death. V had injected himself and this broke the chain of causation.

In **Cato**, D actually injected V so there was no break in the chain of causation. In **Dalby**, V's own act broke the chain.

In **Kennedy 1999**, D mixed the drug and handed the syringe to V and this sufficed even though, as in **Dalby**, V injected himself. In **Dias 2002**, V injected himself, as in **Dalby**. The CA quashed D's conviction on the issue of causation and criticised the decision in **Kennedy**. The conflicting case law led to the Criminal Cases Review Commission referring **Kennedy** back to the CA on the issue of causation. In **Kennedy 2005**, the CA said causing your own death was not unlawful, so nor was encouraging another to. However, participating in the administration of a 'poison' or 'noxious thing' is a crime, and so forms the basis for a manslaughter charge. The case then went to the HL.

**Key case**

In **Kennedy 2007**, the HL quashed the conviction and held that in the case of a fully informed adult self-administering the drug it would never be appropriate to find the supplier guilty of manslaughter. D had not administered the drug and although he had committed an unlawful act in supplying the heroin, this did not cause the victim's death so he was not guilty.

Application of the three essentials can be seen in **Carey and Others 2006**. A teenage girl died from a heart attack following an attack on her and three other girls. The group who carried out the attack were charged with manslaughter. The CA confirmed the three elements, (i) that there was an unlawful act, (ii) which was dangerous in the sense that the unlawful act subjected V to the risk of physical harm, and (iii) that the unlawful act caused her death. As regards the unlawful act, the prosecution relied on the public order offence of 'affray'. This is using or threatening unlawful violence towards another, which would cause a person of reasonable firmness present at the scene to fear for his/her personal safety. The CA confirmed, following **Church**, that 'dangerous' was an objective test. Affray was not dangerous in the required sense because it would not have been recognised by a 'sober and reasonable bystander' that an apparently healthy 15-year-old was at risk of suffering harm as a result. On causation, both **Dawson** and **Watson** were discussed. It was agreed that it was not foreseeable that an apparently healthy man would suffer a heart attack in an attempted robbery (**Dawson**). It was also agreed that it *was* foreseeable that an obviously frail and very old man was at risk of suffering a heart attack during a burglary committed at his home late at night (**Watson**). The current case involved a healthy young girl, so was nearer to **Dawson** than **Watson**. It had been argued that V was running from the attack so, as in **Roberts**, this did not break the chain of causation. However, the CA felt that she was not running away, merely running home, because there was no longer any threat by then. Although V had suffered a punch to her face, an unlawful act, this minor injury did not cause her death. The act of affray was unlawful but not dangerous, so the manslaughter charge failed.

This can be compared to **R v M (J); R v M (S) 2012**, above. A similar violent incident was held to be a substantial cause of the doorman's shock and had significantly contributed to his death. The shock and the increase in blood pressure led to his collapse and an internal rupture, from which he died. Shock was foreseeable, and there was found to be no break in the chain of causation between the violence and the death.

Before going on to *mens rea,* let's recap with an imaginary scenario.

### Example

Vic decides to kill himself and jumps off a tall building, checking before he does so that no one is underneath. Dave is a resident of the building who is having a violent row with his wife. He fires a gun at her and misses, hitting Vic as he passes the window. Vic is thrown off course by the blow and lands on a pedestrian, Sue, killing her. Vic survives. Can anyone be charged with manslaughter?

Look at the three requirements. Vic's act is *dangerous* and *caused her death*, but is not *unlawful*. Vic is unlikely to be found guilty of manslaughter. Dave's act is both *dangerous* and *unlawful*. However, did it *cause death*? Unlikely; Vic's jumping would be the cause and as it was not foreseeable, it would break the chain of causation. Dave is also unlikely to be found guilty of manslaughter.

### Mens rea

There is no special *mens rea* for this type of manslaughter. It is the *mens rea* for the unlawful act. There is therefore no need to prove *mens rea* as regards the death, only for whatever the unlawful act is. Let's take one of the earlier examples a step further.

### Example

Going back to **Nedrick**, the unlawful act was arson, a form of criminal damage. The *mens rea* for this is intent or recklessness. There is no need for D to intend, or to recognise a risk of, death, only to intend or see a risk of the damage. Arson was clearly intended, so *mens rea* was easy to prove for the manslaughter charge to succeed.

To practise for a problem question look at a case you are familiar with and apply the law you have learnt. Let's try this with **Pagett**.

### Summary of how to apply the rules

### Facts:

**1**. D shot at the police whilst holding the girl in front of him.

**2**. The police returned fire.

**3**. The girl was killed.

**Application with cases in support:**

*Actus reus*

There is an unlawful killing, so the first question is whether D caused it.

**'But for'** his action she would not have died (**White**). He factually caused death.

He also made a **'significant contribution'** (**Cheshire**) to the girl's death. The intervening act of the police shooting back was **foreseeable** and so did not break the **chain of causation** (**Roberts**). He legally caused death.

We have *actus reus* but is it murder or manslaughter?

*Mens rea*

Was D's **aim** to **kill or seriously injure** the girl? No, so there is no direct intent. Was death or serious injury a **'virtual certainty'** and did D **appreciate** this (**Nedrick**)? If the jury find this not to be the case there is no indirect intent. However, if the jury believe that D intended to kill or seriously injure the police, whether directly or by appreciating it as a virtual certainty, then the principle of transferred malice means that this intent is transferred from them to the girl and he may be found guilty. In the case, he was found not guilty of murder by the jury due to lack of *mens rea*. If no intent is proved then the conviction will be for manslaughter.

**Examination tip**

It is quite OK to say 'probably' in a conclusion. You can't be expected to play judge and jury. It is better than "D will be guilty (or not) of ..." – it is rarely that simple! Decide what seems most appropriate, and then use the law to prove it. You could say, "D could be charged with murder, but it may be hard to prove intent so a manslaughter charge may be more appropriate". Then go on to discuss involuntary manslaughter.

**Task 4**

Refer to the above application of the law to **Pagett**. Now add the new rules for manslaughter. Keep the whole thing as a guide for problem questions on homicide.

The only other point on *mens rea* is to remember that it must coincide with the *actus reus*. As we saw this is widely interpreted. Thus in both **Thabo Meli** and in **Church**, the Ds were guilty of unlawful and dangerous act manslaughter based on a 'series of acts'.

**Examination tip**

Look for clues in the scenario as to which type of manslaughter is most appropriate. The CA in **Adomako** indicated that it could be gross negligence manslaughter where, e.g., an electrician caused a death by faulty wiring. This was *obiter dicta* because it was not relevant on the facts of the case. It could be referred to if the given scenario involved such circumstances, or something similar. Although not binding, *obiter dicta* can be used as *persuasive precedent*.

Although you won't usually have a scenario based on both types (unless there are two separate situations) be aware that, as we saw in **Willoughby**, the two types of manslaughter do overlap. If you think it is constructive manslaughter, discuss this first, but if, e.g., there is doubt as to whether there is an act or omission, or whether the act is unlawful, go on to gross negligence manslaughter as an alternative. If, as in **Willoughby**, there is some doubt as to whether a duty is owed, you could start with gross negligence manslaughter and go on to constructive manslaughter as an alternative.

**Summary of constructive manslaughter**

| actus reus | • an unlawful act<br>• which is dangerous<br>• which causes death |
|---|---|

| mens rea | • whatever *mens rea* is required for the unlawful act |
|---|---|

## Self-test questions

*Can you commit either type of manslaughter by omission?*

*In what circumstances will an omission amount to* actus reus*?*

*What were the facts and principle in **Church**?*

*At what point was the act deemed dangerous in **Bristow**?*

*At what point was the act deemed dangerous in **Watson**?*

*What did the HL decide in **Kennedy 2007**?*

For some free interactive exercises visit www.drsr.org and click on Free Exercises to see what's available

*A general guide to revision*

The first and foremost rule for revision is to start early. Too many students leave it until the last minute and then get in a panic. If you take it gently and organise your time properly you will feel a lot more calm and confident when exam time comes. Make a plan of what you want to cover each day and try to stick to it. Don't forget to include some breaks in your schedule, if you are tired it will be harder to retain the material you have been revising.

Here are a few tips for revision techniques

> *Go through your notes and try to summarise them*
>
> *Learn the key cases, as these are essential to know*
>
> *Make sure you understand how the judge has applied the law to the facts so you can do the same in an examination scenario*

**Example**

In **Watson 1989**, burglars entered a house and saw an elderly man, but continued with their act of burglary. Their knowledge of the man's frailty could be attributed to the reasonable person who would therefore see the act as dangerous, as required by **Church**. The judge could distinguish **Dawson** on these different facts, so they were guilty of manslaughter

> *Go through the summaries of the topic, these provide a base of the essential points which may need to be addressed*
>
> *Go to the examination board's website for past exam papers, mark schemes and reports*
>
> *Practice answering questions then look at the examiners' mark schemes and reports to see if you were on the right track*

*Revision of involuntary manslaughter*

Manslaughter is the appropriate charge where death has been caused by D but there is no intent to kill or cause serious injury, so any murder charge would fail due to lack of *mens rea*. The two types of manslaughter are gross negligence manslaughter and unlawful act or constructive manslaughter.

Gross negligence manslaughter requires a duty of care, a risk of death, a breach of duty and criminal negligence. The *mens rea* is gross negligence.

**Example**

Mr Jones owns a block of bedsits and he lets out a room to Raphael. The wiring is very old and while Raphael is asleep the electric heating malfunctions and a fire starts. Raphael dies in the fire. Mr Jones, as a landlord, will owe a duty to all his tenants to maintain and manage the building properly. This would be a contractual duty as in **Pittwood;** another example is **Wacker**. He has breached the duty because he has not maintained the wiring, and a reasonable person would have done so, as in **Wacker** where the transporters were guilty for the deaths of the immigrants, as reasonable people would have provided proper ventilation. Any fault in an electrical system will involve a risk of death because it can kill through electric shock or, as in this case, through a fire. In **Adomako,** the CA used the example of faulty wiring in *obiter dicta* to the effect that in such as case an electrician could be guilty of gross negligence manslaughter. Although not binding, this may be a persuasive precedent and be followed here. The jury are likely to find that Mr Jones has acted sufficiently badly for criminal negligence to be established, as he is making money from the property so should have a suitable maintenance programme in place.

Constructive manslaughter requires an unlawful act, which is dangerous and which causes death. The *mens rea* is that for the unlawful act, usually intent or subjective recklessness.

### Example

Viktor and Sergei are having a competition to see who can throw the largest stone onto the roof of a railway carriage as it goes under a bridge. Viktor's stone breaks a window and a piece of glass hits a passenger, severing an artery. The passenger dies on the way to hospital. Viktor is likely to be guilty of constructive manslaughter. The unlawful act is criminal damage as the stone has damaged the window. In these circumstances, it is also a dangerous act, as sober and reasonable people would see it as risking harm to throw stones at a moving train (**Church**). The damage to the window has caused the death because but for Viktor's act of criminal damage, the passenger would not have died (unlike in **White**). The damage made a significant contribution to the death (**Cheshire**) and the chain of causation is not broken, because even if the throwing of the stone did not directly cause death (e.g., by hitting the passenger on the head) it is foreseeable that a window may be broken when throwing stones. This means the breaking of the window and the glass then hitting the passenger would not break the chain (as in **Roberts** where her foreseeable act of jumping out of the car did not break the chain). As regards *mens rea*, this will be easy to establish because Viktor need not have *mens rea* for the death, only the damage. Even if he did not intend damage to occur he must have foreseen the risk of it and he went ahead with his actions so has subjective recklessness, as established in **Cunningham**

### Self-test questions

*Why was D not convicted in **Lamb**?*

*What test came from **Church**?*

*What happened in **Cato**?*

*Why was Cato convicted but not Dalby?*

*What was the unlawful act in **Hancock & Shankland**?*

*What main elements are required for gross negligence manslaughter?*

*Which case confirmed that a risk of death is needed?*

*What three main elements are required for the* actus reus *of constructive manslaughter?*

*What is the* mens rea *of constructive manslaughter?*

### Examination tip

Remember that, although you won't usually have a scenario based on both types (unless there are two separate situations), the two types of manslaughter do overlap. Look for clues in the scenario as to which seems most appropriate and then go on to the other type if necessary.

### Example

In **Willoughby 2004**, D recruited the taxi driver so owed him a duty of care as someone who would be affected by his actions. He had breached this by asking him to help to set the fire and not taking care that the building, which he owned, was safe. There is a risk of death in a situation where a fire is started inside a building.  Whether his negligence was sufficiently gross to be deemed criminal is arguable either way but a conviction is quite possible.  However, the fact that arson is unlawful makes constructive manslaughter the more appropriate charge.  D had committed the unlawful act of arson, and this is likely to be seen as dangerous by 'reasonable and sober people' (**Church**).  He clearly had *mens rea* for arson because he intended to set the fire.  He did not need to have *mens rea* for the death, only the arson, remember.  The unlawful act caused death because but for D's act in asking for help in setting the fire, death would not have occurred (**White**).  He also made a significant contribution to the death by helping to set the fire (**Cheshire**), and there were no intervening acts to break the chain of causation because a building collapsing after being set on fire is foreseeable (**Roberts**).

On appeal, the CA said that the judge should have directed the jury on unlawful act manslaughter rather than gross negligence manslaughter.  They made it clear that either may be appropriate, depending on the circumstances.  However as D had committed an unlawful act, and this caused death, the manslaughter conviction was upheld.

**Task 5**

**Refer back to the case of Evans and then answer the following questions**

*Which type of manslaughter was she charged with?  Give reasons for your answer with case(s) in support*

*What are the main elements of this charge and in which two cases were they established and restated?*

*Using cases in support, apply the law to the given facts to come to a reasoned conclusion as to why D was guilty of manslaughter.*

For some free interactive exercises visit www.drsr.org and click on Free Exercises to see what's available

Although different exam boards have different ways of styling their examination papers, there are always going to be common elements. You will need to be able to apply the law you have learnt to a particular scenario and come to a conclusion on liability as appropriate.

### A general guide to examination papers

Read **all** questions carefully before deciding which to answer.

Look again at the ones you wish to answer to make sure you can do so, make brief notes - this can be a useful checklist later when you are tired and your memory begins to fail.

Structure your answer. Remember this is a test of law so you need to state the legal principles involved and apply them to the particular question. A solid start is worth a lot and gets the examiner on your side. A small plan is helpful.

It is necessary to do more than regurgitate your notes. You need to be selective as to what is relevant, and to choose appropriate cases and examples in support of what you say.

Never put in irrelevant material just because you know it - there is **never** a question asking you to 'write all you know about...'. The examiner wants to know that you understand the specific issues and can apply the appropriate law to the facts given.

Always support your answer with **relevant** cases. Don't worry too much about the facts, the principle forming the *ratio decidendi* is usually the important part e.g. in **Donoghue v Stevenson** that you owe a duty to others to take care is vital but you don't need to write a paragraph discussing snails and ginger beer.

Having said that, you want to show why you have chosen a particular case so will need to mention any facts that specifically relate to the scenario. If the scenario mentions someone being ill after consuming a chocolate bar with a dead mouse in it (yes, there has been a case!) then talking briefly about snails in ginger beer will be relevant. The main point here is that you need to be selective; this demonstrates a skill in itself and conserves precious time.

If you can't remember the name of a case that is relevant, don't leave it out but refer to it in a general way e.g. 'in one decided case....' or 'in a similar case....'

Aim for a logical structure when applying the law. Identify the various issues in the first paragraph and then set about dealing with them one by one, applying the relevant law and cases to each issue, **referring to the facts of the question as you do so**. This tells the examiner that you are answering the specific points raised. A short summing up is also a good idea e.g., "In conclusion it would appear that D may be liable for ... but it is possible that the defence of ... applies which will reduce/negate liability".

### Examination practice for involuntary manslaughter

### Problem scenarios (application)

The law on *actus reus* and *mens rea* prepares you for answering problem questions on this topic.

Gross negligence manslaughter can be committed by an omission (**Stone and Dobinson, Pittwood** etc.). Constructive manslaughter cannot be through an omission (**Khan**). Both types of manslaughter are result crimes because death must result from the act or omission. Therefore, D's act or omission must have caused death actually (**White**) and in law (**Cheshire**). Constructive manslaughter requires the *mens rea* of intent (**Nedrick/Woollin**) to commit the unlawful act, or subjective recklessness (**Cunningham**) to cause it.

## Examination tip

Application of the law requires you to be selective. The facts should point you to particular issues which need addressing and you must be prepared to pick out the relevant law and cases and to leave out anything irrelevant – for which you will gain no marks.

## Example

Pete has a violent argument with his neighbour Tom. He is very angry, so he goes next door later that night and cuts down Tom's favourite tree, a large conifer near the house. As it falls, it hits the roof of Tom's house. The roof caves in and kills Tom who is asleep in the room below.

Here there is clearly no *mens rea* for murder so there is no need to discuss this, merely state that as he did not have intent even to seriously injure Pete it will not be murder and go straight on to discuss constructive manslaughter. The act is unlawful as it is criminal damage and again there is no problem in proving *mens rea* so just state clearly that *mens rea* is for the unlawful act and that it is shown by the fact that Tom intended to damage the tree. Go on to mention that the act must also be dangerous so that 'sober and reasonable people' would see the risk of it causing some harm (**Church**). This is not quite so clear, but note the words "near the house"; it is likely that the majority of people would see that cutting down a large tree near to someone's house could harm anyone in the vicinity. The main focus of your answer needs to be on causation. There is firstly a question of whether Tom's act made a significant contribution to Pete's death as required by **Cheshire**. It probably did, because the act need not be the sole cause of the death. Therefore, if Tom's act is significant this is enough, even if there are other causes as well, such as the tree falling. The second question is whether the tree falling onto the house broke the chain of causation between Tom's unlawful act of damaging the tree and Pete's death. It is not likely to break the chain, as it is foreseeable that cutting down a large tree can cause damage to a nearby house and harm to anyone inside it. It was stated in **Roberts** that a foreseeable event would not break the chain. In conclusion, Pete is likely to be found guilty of (constructive) manslaughter. His act was both unlawful and dangerous and he intended the damage so has *mens rea*. Also, 'but for' his act in cutting down the tree Tom would not have died, he made a significant enough contribution to Tom's death and the chain of causation was not broken by the foreseeable event of the tree falling on the house.

## Examination tip

It is **good practice** to be selective. Select only the law that applies to the given facts. This shows that you understand the law well enough to know what is relevant.

It is **bad practice** to write all you know about an area just because you know it well. Even if it is right, you will gain no marks if it is not relevant to the facts given.

There is limited time in most exams and examiners rarely set a question which requires you to cover everything. To practise being selective do the following exercise.

## Task 6 Clue spotting – application practice

Look at the brief comments taken from the scenarios and state what they indicate is the focus of the question with cases in support, adding which type of manslaughter seems most appropriate if the victim dies. The first one is done for you as an example.

**Winston gave Joe some heroin and when Joe injected himself, he used too much and died from an overdose**

The focus here is on causation. The cases of **Cato** and **Dalby** show the difference between supplying a drug and assisting in the taking of it. From the case of **Kennedy** we can conclude that the unlawful act did not cause death because the HL held that, in the case of an adult, it would not be right to find a supplier of drugs guilty of manslaughter if the victim self-administers the drug. The appropriate charge would be unlawful act manslaughter but it would fail on this point, unless the victim was a child.

**Jake threw a book at Jon which hit him on the shoulder. Unfortunately, Jon suffered from a disease which meant that any slight bruise caused internal bleeding**

**The electrician wired the switch wrongly and the householder was electrocuted**

**Mario threatened to hit Ahmed who jumped back in fright and fell onto an old woman who had brittle bones**

**Mark hit his girlfriend causing a sprained wrist. She went to hospital where the doctor failed to ask if she was allergic to any drugs and gave her a large dose of painkillers, to which she had a fatal reaction**

In all problem questions, you need to take a logical approach. First, read the facts carefully to ensure that you understand the points raised by the scenario. Then apply the relevant law in a logical manner, using cases in support. All exam questions can be approached in a similar way. Use the following as a guide.

   Identify the law (what is the appropriate charge in each case?).

   State the law; define either or both types of manslaughter as appropriate.

   Manslaughter is a result crime (the result being a death), so causation is very important.

   Apply the law: Are the requirements of manslaughter met? Has death been caused? Did D's act cause it? What is the *mens rea* and did D have it?

   Reach a conclusion based on your application in each case.

As practice for an exam question, try this with the following scenario

**Task 7 Problem scenario - application practice**

Read the facts and then use your knowledge of the *actus reus* and *mens rea* of manslaughter to apply the law to these facts.

Marie took her five-year old son Jacques to the lake for a picnic. She drank a bottle of wine and fell asleep. Jacques wandered off and saw some older boys playing on a bridge over the lake. When he tried to join in, they chased him away and one of them, Chas, picked up a stick and threatened him. Jacques was scared and ran away but he fell off the bridge and into the water. The water was deep at this point and he drowned.
Discuss the possible liability of both Marie and Chas for Jacques' death.

Note that there are no evaluation (essay) questions on this topic.

Task 1

A duty of responsibility was seen in **Stone and Dobinson**, and was breached by not taking sufficient care of a relative.

A contractual duty was seen in **Pittwood**, breached by not doing his job, which was closing the gate.

Task 2 - this is covered in the chapter itself but repeated here

The unlawful act is different for each case and added below, for causation in fact and in law it must be shown that

> *'but for' D's conduct the victim would not have died (causation in fact)*
>
> *D made a significant contribution*
>
> *nothing broke the chain of causation (causation in law)*

These are applied below.

**Hancock and Shankland (1986)**

> Throwing the stone is criminal damage. The driver would not have died 'but for' D throwing the stone and throwing the stone made a significant contribution to the death.

**Pagett (1983)**

> Shooting at the police is assault; 'but for' D shooting at the police the girl would not have died. Shooting at the police made a significant contribution to the death and the police firing back was foreseeable so did not break the chain of causation.

**Nedrick (1986)**

> Setting the fire is arson, a type of criminal damage; 'but for' the fire the victim would not have died and the fire made a significant contribution to the death.

Task 3

**Risk of death**: It is known that ecstasy can kill so there is a risk of death.

**Duty:** they owed her a duty as a visitor and/or as a child in their care.

**Breach**: They did not call an ambulance for some time so they had breached their duty to her by not taking reasonable care.

**Gross negligence**: The jury may think that the fact that they had hidden the tablets, and they had attempted to treat her meant that their actions were not sufficiently gross to amount to criminal liability. If this is the case then, although they breached their duty, they will not be guilty of manslaughter.

In the case itself, the jury found that they had not shown a sufficiently high level of negligence to be deemed criminal so they were not guilty of gross negligence manslaughter.

Task 4

The *actus reus* for murder and manslaughter is pretty much the same. It mostly involves proving that the act caused the death so when applying the law on involuntary manslaughter to the facts of **Pagett** you can refer back to any earlier discussion of murder for the causation part. Then go on to say that the unlawful act must not only cause death, but also be dangerous in that sober and reasonable people would see the risk of some harm resulting (**Church**). Firing a gun is clearly a dangerous act. *Mens rea* for manslaughter is for the act itself, there is no need to have *mens rea* as regards the death. The unlawful act is a minimum of assault, and the *mens rea* for this is intent or subjective recklessness to cause the victim to fear immediate harm. Pagett must have recognised that pointing and firing a gun at someone risked causing fear to that person. He was therefore at least subjectively reckless because knowing of the risk he went ahead anyway.

## Examination tip

There are several crimes that Pagett may have committed here and sometimes you may be unsure what the unlawful act is and therefore what the *mens rea* is. This may be the case, e.g., if the scenario involves criminal damage and you have not studied this area. If so, don't worry. Just explain that the *mens rea* will be intent or subjective recklessness for the unlawful act and go on to say that as long as D foresaw the risk of the consequences of the unlawful act (whether this is criminal damage, assault or some other crime) then *mens rea* will be proved. One further tip – the unlawful act must cause death so you cannot use, e.g., having an unlicensed gun as the having of the gun did not cause death (as in **Kennedy** where the supply of the drug was unlawful but was not the cause of death)

Self-test questions

*You can commit gross negligence manslaughter by omission (but not constructive manslaughter – **Khan**)*

*An omission can amount to actus reus where there is a duty of care*

*In **Church** D believed the woman to be dead when he threw her in the river and so argued that the act was not dangerous, as it isn't dangerous to throw a dead person in the river. The principle was that it was not what D believed that mattered, if sober and reasonable people would see that throwing a woman into a river was dangerous this was enough*

*The act was deemed dangerous in **Bristow** at the start of the burglary*

*The act was deemed dangerous in **Watson** when it was seen that the householder was old and frail*

*The HL decided in **Kennedy 2007** that it would never be appropriate to hold a supplier of drugs guilty of manslaughter in the case of an adult who self-injected*

## Self-test questions - Revision

*There was no unlawful act in **Lamb***

*The test for whether the act is dangerous is objective, based on what reasonable and sober people would deem dangerous*

*D supplied heroin to the victim and helped him inject it; the victim died*

*Because in **Cato** there was a positive act; he helped him inject the drug. In **Dalby** he merely supplied the drug and did not help him to inject it*

*Criminal damage*

*A risk of death, a duty of care, breach of duty and sufficient gross negligence*

***Misra***

*An unlawful act, which is dangerous and which causes death*

## Task 5

The charge was gross negligence manslaughter.  Unlawful act manslaughter would be less likely to succeed because V self-injected, so there was no unlawful act (the supply did not cause the death) (**Kennedy**).   In addition, an omission (to get medical help) is not enough for unlawful act manslaughter.  It was held in **Khan** that an omission cannot apply to unlawful act manslaughter but can apply to gross negligence manslaughter if there is a duty of care.  **Stone & Dobinson** and **Gibbins & Proctor** both involved a duty of care to a relative.  A duty also arises from creating a dangerous situation as in **Miller**.  All these points suggest that gross negligence manslaughter is the appropriate charge.

The main elements of this charge are that there is a risk of death, a duty of care, a breach of that duty which amounted to gross negligence, and the negligence was a substantial cause of death.  The test was established in **Adomako** and restated in **Misra 2004**.

Applying the test from **Adomako**, although her mother would owe a duty of care due to relationship as in **Gibbins and Proctor,** the duty is not as clear for D because she is only a half-sister, not a parent.  Although no duty was found between a dealer and his client in **Khan,** the facts here are a little different and the charge can be supported by other cases.  **Stone and Dobinson** could support an argument for a duty based on a voluntary assumption of responsibility for another person who is not a close relative.  The facts here are similar because again nothing was done to get medical help.  In **Evans**, the CA held that a duty was not confined to close family relationships but also said that if a person created, or contributed to, a situation which was life threatening then a duty to take reasonable steps to save that life would arise.  D had created a state of affairs which she knew (or should have known) had become life threatening.  This is similar to the duty in **Miller** where he had created a situation where there was a risk of fire and did nothing to eliminate that risk.  Here D bought the heroin and gave it to V, so can be said to have created a risky situation, and nothing was done to eliminate the risk, e.g., by getting medical help.  The Court of Appeal made clear in **Misra** that there must also be a risk of death.  Here there is a risk of death because she had overdosed and neither D nor her mother attempted to get medical help.  On the facts given, the duty appears to have been breached because D's actions did not reach the standard of the reasonable person, a reasonable person would get medical help.  The final step is to decide if D's actions were sufficiently bad to be seen as 'grossly negligent', i.e., her conduct was so bad in all the circumstances as to amount to a criminal act or omission.  This is a matter for the jury so could be argued either way.  In conclusion, if the jury agree her conduct was sufficiently bad to be deemed criminal, D is guilty of manslaughter, and this appears to be the case as she was convicted.  Her appeal is unlikely to succeed because there appears to be supporting case law for the finding of a duty, and this is what she appealed on.

## Task 6 Clue spotting – application practice

**Jake threw a book at Jon which hit him on the shoulder.  Unfortunately, Jon suffered from a disease which meant that any slight bruise caused internal bleeding.**

The focus here is on the 'thin skull' rule (**Blaue**).  This means Jake must take Jon as he finds him and the fact that someone without the disease would not have died will not affect his liability for the resulting death.  The appropriate charge is constructive manslaughter as throwing the book is a battery.  He clearly had *mens rea* for this unlawful act, as it only requires intent or subjective recklessness to apply force on another. He seems to have direct intent as he threw the book 'at' Jon, but even if not, he must have seen the risk of a battery occurring and went ahead anyway so was subjectively reckless.

**The electrician wired the switch wrongly and the householder was electrocuted.**

The focus here is on gross negligence manslaughter; the electrician has not committed an unlawful act, so no marks can be gained for discussing constructive manslaughter. However, in **Adomako** there were *obiter dicta* to the effect that such a situation would be gross negligence manslaughter. The electrician will owe a duty to the householder. He has breached that duty by not doing his job properly as in **Pittwood**.

**Mario threatened to hit Ahmed who jumped back in fright and fell onto an old woman who had brittle bones.**

The focus here is on transferred malice. The *mens rea* of assault on Ahmed can be transferred to the resulting death of the woman (**Latimer**). The appropriate charge is constructive manslaughter. Assault is unlawful and usually seen as dangerous. The only *mens rea* required is that he intended or was subjectively reckless as to causing fear (in respect of Ahmed), and this should not be hard to prove.

**Mark hit his girlfriend causing a sprained wrist. She went to hospital where the doctor failed to ask if she was allergic to any drugs and gave her a large dose of painkillers. She was allergic to these and suffered a reaction to the drugs from which she died.**

The focus here is on causation. Hospital treatment does not usually break the chain of causation unless it is independent of the original act (**Cheshire**). As she only had a sprained wrist, it is likely that in this case the chain is broken because Mark's act is not a significant cause of death. This means that even though 'but for' his original act she would not have gone to hospital and so not have died, Mark will not be liable for her death because legal causation is not proven. The appropriate charge will be gross negligence manslaughter against the doctor. He owes a duty to all patients. He has breached that duty by not taking sufficient care in a situation which carries a risk of death.

### Task 7 Problem scenario - application practice

As regards Marie, the charge will be manslaughter. She has not acted unlawfully, so it is not constructive manslaughter. The most appropriate charge for Marie would be gross negligence manslaughter. This requires a duty of care, a risk of death, a breach of duty and gross negligence, as established in **Adomako**. A mother owes a duty of care to her child, even a non-family member can be owed a duty as in **Stone and Dobinson**, so there no problem establishing a duty. In **Misra**, the CA confirmed there must be a risk of death not just harm. Jacques is very young so it is likely that this is satisfied because they are by the lake and the water is deep. Marie has breached her duty because a reasonable person would not drink wine and fall asleep when with such a young child. The jury would have to decide if her negligence was sufficiently gross to be deemed criminal. This is debatable. In **Wood & Hodgson** the jury did not think leaving ecstasy tablets for a ten-year old to find, and then not calling an ambulance for some time, was enough and this could be the case here. There is also a causation issue because Jacques did not just wander off and fall in the lake because she was not looking after him; Chas caused him to do this by threatening him. Although two people can be liable for the same death, it is possible that Chas' actions have broken the chain of causation between the breach of duty by Marie and the death of her son. In **Cheshire**, it was said that an act could break the chain if it was 'independent' of D's act and a 'potent cause' in itself. This is probably the case here, so even though it can be said that she factually caused death, because but for her negligence he would not have wandered off and therefore not have died (**White**), any charge is likely to fail on legal causation as her omission to take care did not make a significant contribution to the boy's death.

This brings us to Chas' liability for the death. Here unlawful act manslaughter is the appropriate charge. This requires an unlawful act which is dangerous and causes death. Chas has threatened Jacques and caused him to be in fear so there is an unlawful act, specifically assault. Threatening a child with a stick is likely to be seen as dangerous by 'sober and reasonable people' as required by **Church**, even if it was not near deep water which makes it more dangerous. There is a small causation issue because Chas did not directly cause the death. However, according to **Roberts**, a foreseeable act by the victim, such as running away from a threat, will not break the chain of causation. The only thing that might do is where the victim does something 'daft' and it is not at all daft for a child to run away from an older boy with a stick. There is no problem proving *mens rea* because the only *mens rea* needed is that for the assault, and it is clear that even if Chas argued he did not intend to frighten Jacques he would certainly have seen the risk of doing so. As he went ahead with his threatening behaviour knowing of this risk, he would have subjective (**Cunningham**) recklessness to causing Jacques to fear harm, and this is enough.

In conclusion, Maria is likely to be acquitted if charged with manslaughter but Chas is likely to be found guilty.

www.ingramcontent.com/pod-product-compliance
Lightning Source LLC
Chambersburg PA
CBHW051421170526
45165CB00004BA/1916